I0152319

HEAVENLY ANGEL

LAY LAY

EXPLAINS WHY

GAYS, LESBIANS
BI-SEXUALS
AND TRANSSEXUALS

DO NOT

GO TO HEAVEN

PUBLISHING COMPANY

Published by Crossover Ministries; Walter@crossover-ministries-publishing.com Copyright 2007. All rights reserved. Any and all reproduction of any type; including email, recording, printing of this book or contents herein, etc. is strictly prohibited by Federal Law without prior written permission. No part of this or any other publication made by Crossover Ministries may be reproduced, stored in any type of transmittal system or retrieval system in any form or by any means electronically, mechanically, or otherwise, without the prior written permission of Walter Burchett, BA. Violators will be prosecuted in Federal Court. This book and all its contents is Copyrighted by World Intellectual Property Organization (WIPO) in 23 different treaties all around the world, including the International Property Protection (IP-Protection) Berne Convention, Brussels Convention, Madrid Agreement, Nairobi Treaty, Paris Convention, Rome Convention, and Washington Treaty. The Copyright covers 189 different countries. Global Protection System (GPS) includes the Budapest Treaty, Haque Agreement, Lisbon Agreement, Madrid Agreement, Madrid Protocol, PCT, WCT, and WPPT. The Classification covers Locarno Agreement, Nice Agreement, Strasborg Agreement, and Vienna Agreement.

Copyright 2007 Walter Burchett, BA All Rights Reserved.

ISBN: 978-0-6151-7485-3

www.crossover-ministries-publishing.com

TABLE OF CONTENTS

1. About the Author   4
2. Introduction   5

GAYS, LESBIANS, BI-SEXUALS TRANSSEXUALS

3. Gays, Lesbians, Bi-Sexuals, Transsexuals   7

JACOB AND JOSEPH

4. Jacob and Joseph   17

MOSES

5. Moses   43

BIBLIOGRAPHY

6. Bibliography   49

ABOUT THE AUTHOR

I was dedicated to Jesus Christ of Nazareth as an infant and accepted Him as my Lord and Savior around seven years old when a visiting youth group led me in prayer at the alter. During my Salvation Prayer I asked Jesus to use me in a special ministry. Something that very few other Christians would want to do. I saw all the people just sitting in the pews, the ushers, and the Sunday School teachers and realized any Christian could do that. I wanted something different. One day in church service there was a visiting minister at a church I was visiting as well. The Minister said, "Jesus is going to make you a 'Healer of a Heart'". Then he asked me if I knew what that meant. I said, "No." the minister said, "I don't either, but whatever it is, Jesus is going to use you in a powerful way.

Helping Rachael, Jesus showed me what a 'Healer of the Heart' is. During the course of me helping Rachael to the 'Promised Land', a real Heavenly Angel named Lay Lay and I were allowed one hour one day to talk about Spiritual and Family situations from the King James Version of the Word of God. These books are designed to answer a lot of Spiritual Questions not even your minister can answer or your Church Denomination. I know theology Doctors who can't tell you how people other than Noah and his family made it past the 'Great Flood', yet their names are listed in the King James Version of the Word of God right after the 'World Wide Flood'. These books explain that and much more. I have written these books to tell the whole truth about the Word of God no matter how difficult it may be for me or others. Yes, there are things I write in these books that I don't even like, but in all fairness and total honestly, I must say the WHOLE TRUTH. The title of this book is 100% real. HEAVENLY ANGEL LAY LAY explained to me why gays, lesbians, bi-sexuals, and transsexuals DO NOT go to Heaven. I know this may make some people mad, but I won't 'Candy Coat' the Word of the Living God or what any Heavenly Angel said to me.

INTRODUCTION

The first section of this book talks about gays, lesbians, bi-sexuals, transvestites, and transsexuals, tells you how they became that way and why **GAYS, LESBIANS, BI-SEXUALS, TRANSVESTITES, AND TRANSSEXUALS DO NOT GO TO HEAVEN** and why it's not a judgment call to say they won't be going to Heaven. The second section of this book tells about Jacob and Joseph. All scriptures are taken from the King James Version of the Word of God. This book contains an excerpt from my book. MATTHEW'S WORD 'TWO':REAL WORD OF GOD BIBLE.

BOOKS WRITTEN BY WALTER BURCHETT, BA:

MATTHEW'S WORD 'TWO':REAL WORD OF GOD BIBLE   ISBN: 1-4116-6995-9

HEAVENLY ANGEL LAY LAY EXPLAINS WHY ADAM WAS NEVER CURSED
          ISBN: 978-1-84728-176-0

HEAVENLY ANGEL LAY LAY EXPLAINS WHY ABORTED BABIES DO NOT GO TO HEAVEN
          ISBN: 978-0-6151-7470-9

HEAVENLY ANGEL LAY LAY EXPLAINS THE BIBLICAL GROUNDS FOR MARRIAGE,
          SEPARATION, AND DIVORCE   ISBN: 978-0-6151-7481-5

HEAVENLY ANGEL LAY LAY EXPLAINS WHY PROFESSIONAL COUNSELORS HAVE 'HARDENED
          HEARTS'   ISBN: 978-0-6151-7482-2

HEAVENLY ANGEL LAY LAY EXPLAINS THE DIFFERENCE BETWEEN A 'COLD CHRISTIAN' AND
          A 'BACKSLIDER'   ISBN: 978-0-6151-7483-9

HEAVENLY ANGEL LAY LAY EXPLAINS WHICH BIBLE TO READ, WHICH BIBLE NOT TO READ,
          AND WHY   ISBN: 978-0-6151-7484-6

HEAVENLY ANGEL LAY LAY EXPLAINS WHY GAYS, LESBIANS, BI-SEXUALS, AND
          TRANSSEXUALS DO NOT GO TO HEAVEN   ISBN: 978-0-6151-7485-3

HEAVENLY ANGEL LAY LAY EXPLAINS WHY CHILDREN AND SPORTS ARE DEFINITELY A
          RELIGION IN TODAY'S SOCIETY   ISBN: 978-0-6151-7486-0

HEAVENLY ANGEL LAY LAY EXPLAINS WHAT 'MANY ARE CALLED, BUT FEW ARE CHOSEN
          REALLY MEANS   ISBN: 978-0-6151-7487-7

HEAVENLY ANGEL LAY LAY AND GUARDIAN ANGEL SHADOW GUESS THE REAL AGE OF THE
          EARTH   ISBN: 978-0-6151-7488-4

AN ABUSED MAN'S BATTLES, TRYING TO PROTECT HIS BOYS   ISBN: 978-0-6151-5191-5

HEAVENLY ANGEL

LAY LAY

EXPLAINS WHY

GAYS, LESBIANS
BI-SEXUALS
AND TRANSSEXUALS

<u>DO NOT</u>

GO TO HEAVEN

(Heavenly Angel Lay Lay and I were allowed to talk one day for about an hour on different subjects in the King James Version of the Word of God and life on earth. This is an excerpt from my book MATTHEW'S WORD 'TWO':REAL WORD OF GOD BIBLE)

I asked, "What are the roles or characteristics of a Fallen Angel compared to the roles or characteristics of a Heavenly Angel?" Lay Lay said, "The characteristics of a Fallen Angel is 180% opposite as a Heavenly Angel." I asked, "How do Protecting Angels get their appointed vessels to protect?" Lay Lay said, "They have specific Boundary Lines they have to follow." I questioned, "Boundary Lines? I have been from one end of the United States to another and my body doesn't feel any different when I go over the state lines of any state." Lay Lay said, "No, not those Physical Boundary Lines. Going from one state to another or one country to another isn't going to change anything. That's done through the Boundary Lines of the Family Tree of the vessels, the Physical Bloodline." I asked, "We have Guardian Angels. Is there any specific characteristics for our particular angel?" Lay Lay answered, "Yes, Guardian Angels are found under 'Protecting Angels', 'messengers', and 'sons of God' in the Word of God. Each Protecting Angel has a characteristic that is needed to counter the problem that human was born with. You see, everyone was born with at least one thing they need to work on in their life, that's how God made humans. That human's Guardian Angel has the characteristic that helps the human control their particular problem. Take yourself; you have a problem settling down. You were born that way. Your Guardian Angel's name is Sheeya, she goes everywhere with you saying her name, Sssssssshhhhhhhhhhheya, reminding you to settle yourself down and don't get overly anxious. You can hear her in your subconscious, just not your conscious mind. If you were to hear her, all you would hear is Sssssssshhhhhhhhhhhhh. She is always telling you to take your time and don't let anyone force you to hurry. Don't make quick decisions if you can help it. Don't take short-cuts by peer-pressure, etc." About a year after this happened, I was diagnosed with ADHD/ADD, meaning I am hyper and have been since I was born. I didn't know it when I was talking to Lay Lay. I said,

"Revelation talks about demons being cast into Hell for all eternity." Lay Lay said, "Yes, that's true. That's on Judgment Day, until that time they have a second chance to ask forgiveness just like all God's other creation who are still eligible." I asked, "What do you mean 'eligible'?" Lay Lay said, "Satan, the 'sons of God', nor the humans of Sodom, Gomorrah or the other cities God destroyed." I asked, "What happened to the angels for taking the 'daughters of man' for their wives anyway?" Lay Lay said, "What happened is they committed an abomination.

Genesis 6:1-4 (JKV)

1) And it came to pass, when men began to multiply on the face of the Earth, and daughters were born unto them,

2) That the 'sons of God' saw the daughters of men that they *were* fair; and they took them wives of all which they chose.

3) And the Lord said, My spirit shall not always strive with man, for that he also *is* flesh: yet his days shall be an hundred and twenty years.

4) There were giants in the earth in those days: and also after that, when the 'sons of God' came in unto the daughters of men, and they bare *children* to them, the same *became* mighty men which *were* of old, men of renown". They are the ones who are already bound in total darkness waiting for Judgment Day to be judged.

In II Peter 2:4, 5 (KJV)

4) 'For if **God spared not the angels that sinned**, but cast *them* down to hell, and delivered *them* into chains of darkness, to be reserved unto judgment;

5) And spared not the old world, but saved Noah the eighth *person*, a preacher of righteousness, bringing in the flood upon the world of the ungodly;'

Jude 6 (KJV) 'And the **angels** which kept not their first estate (Inheritance of Heaven), but left their own habitation (Original place of living.), he hath reserved in everlasting chains under darkness unto the judgment of the great day'."

I asked, "You mean there were 'two separate falls of angels' from Heaven?" Lay Lay said, "In a manner of speaking. The first one everyone knows about, the Battle in Heaven. The second one is the 'sons of God' or 'Protecting Angels' falling." I said, "The angels weren't warned it was wrong for them to take the 'daughters of man'. Why did God punish them if they didn't know?" Lay Lay said, "They knew:

In Genesis 1:24, 25 (KJV)

24) And God said, Let the earth bring forth the living creature after his kind, cattle, and creeping thing, and beast of the earth after his kind: and it was so.

25) And God made the beast of the earth after his kind, and cattle after their kind, and every thing that creepeth upon the earth after his kind: and God saw that *it was* good.

Genesis 2:18-20 (KJV)

18) And God said, *It* is not good that man should be alone; I will make him an help meet for him.

19) And out of the ground the Lord God formed every beast of the field, and every fowl of the air; and brought *them* unto Adam to see what he would call them: and whatsoever Adam called every living creature, that *was* the name thereof.

20) And Adam gave names to all the cattle, and to the fowl of the air, and to every beast of the field; but for Adam there was not found an help meet for him."

Lay Lay continued, "God told everyone. If there were any Female Heavenly Angels that were good to be Adam's 'help meet' then it would have been so right then and Eve wouldn't have been created to begin with, but there weren't. The Heavenly Angel's job is to 'protect' or 'guard' the humans, not to marry them and have children with them. If there weren't any Female Heavenly Angels good enough to be Adam's 'Personal Assistant', there certainly weren't any Male Heavenly Angels meant to be with human women. Eve was created specifically to be Adam's 'Personal Assistant' and fell to Satan's temptation, now women are to be in submission to men, and women are to 'desire' to do as men tell them according to the King James Version of the Word of God." I asked, "Are there any names of Female Heavenly Angels found in the King James Version of the Word of God?" Lay Lay said, "There are the characteristics of Female Demons in the King James Version of the Word of God. Particular types and strengths of Male Heavenly Angels are above those same types and strengths of Female Heavenly Angels and particular types and strengths of Male Demons are above those same types and strengths of Female Demons as man is above woman. The same reason that women are not listed in the Old and New Testaments unless that specific woman had an important role either for or against the Kingdom of Heaven. Just like everything else, you need to look for the characteristics, not the titles. The characteristics of Female Demons are in the King James Version of the Word of God, like Jezebel, Sodom, Gomorrah, and Mary Magdalene before Mary Magdalene accepted Jesus as her Lord and Savior, all those are the characteristics of a Female Sex Demon, the characteristics of the adulteress. Even though the names of the particular Female Demons are not mentioned, the characteristics are. Now since those are the characteristics of a Female Demon, then that particular Female Demon must have been an Female Heavenly Angel before the fall. The 'sons of God' were Male Heavenly Angels, they took women for their wives. That should tell humans that even if the 'good and evil characteristics' is 180% reversed for a demon that the sexual preference is not, the Female Demon will still prefer the male human to have sex with and in order to get that, the Female Demon will prefer to live in the female human vessel to get the male human for sex. If the Female Demon can't get a female human vessel, then she will go into a male human vessel and change the male characteristics to her own characteristics, that's what humans call gays, transvestites, and transsexuals. The Male Sex Demon in a female vessel would be the characteristics of a lesbian, transvestites, and transsexual. The human feels like they are a man in a woman's body or a woman in a man's body because of the Male or Female Demonic Characteristics in the vessel." I asked, "What about a transvestite?" Lay Lay said, "For you to understand, a transvestite may not be to the same degree that a transsexual is. There are transvestites who would be in the same category as a transsexual and there are other transvestites who are not to that degree yet, but eventually will be, like the boy who was playing with the Satanic Toys, Jesus said, 'It's just a matter of time before he is possessed by an 'unclean spirit.' A bi-sexual, for a human woman, is usually the first step in the sequence of events to a lesbian. For a human male it's usually a transvestite 'Cross Dresser' and then a transsexual and actually changing their sex, the demonic characteristics take over the human mind and heart and the demonic characteristics start going through the human vessel instead of the human characteristics so the human honestly believe they were born in the wrong sexual body. The demonic powers make the human change not only their sexual preference from what the human was really born with, but their human anatomy as well. No man made law or operation is going to change any human's real sex, the sex the human was created with when their soul, spirit, and sperm went into the egg is their real sex. God told the humans again in Leviticus 18:22 and 23: (KJV)

22) Thou shalt not lie with mankind, as with womankind: it is abomination.

23) Neither shalt thou lie with any beast to defile thyself therewith: neither shall any woman stand before a beast to lie down thereto: it is abomination."

Lay Lay continued, "In essence what God is saying in all these verses is that it is an abomination for any of His creation that have not fallen, such as an animal and a human or an angel and a human or an angel and an animal to mate with anyone or anything different than that particular type or species of creation and even then, only with the opposite sex." I asked, "What about Lillith trying to seduce me?" Lay Lay said, "Lillith is an 'unclean spirit' now and she would not marry you anyway. Yes she is God's creation, but she would have changed the body to whatever you wanted. That's Lillith's job now that she serves Satan, 180% opposite Jesus. The 'sons of God' were manifesting themselves as their true form when this happened. That's how the humans knew they were the 'sons of God' to begin with and how there came to be giants on Earth. If they were demons, the Word of God would have said, 'devils' and not 'sons of God'. Moses would have used the term, 'devils' for Fallen Angels, not 'sons of God' for angels. Moses signified the 'sons of God' were not the Fallen Angels.

In Leviticus 17:7 (KJV) And they shall no more offer their sacrifices unto **devils**, after whom they have gone a whoring. This shall be a statue for ever unto them throughout their generation.

Deuteronomy 32:17 (KJV) They sacrificed unto **devils**, not to God; to gods whom they knew not, to new *gods that* came newly up, whom your fathers feared not."

Lay Lay said, "The humans wouldn't have known anything about it, the demon doesn't manifest themselves to humans for that purpose and the offspring would have been human offspring, not giants, just like a human possessed by a sex demon today. Fallen angels wouldn't have wanted to marry to begin with, it's against the character of Satan for humans to marry anyone in the Physical World, except in the case of keeping the Proper Physical Bloodline clean which God commands, so Satan has to obey that. Satanists are married to Satan in the Spiritual World, but not the Physical World. Gabriella wanted her people to marry, but the Anti-Christ put a stop to most of her new laws. The Sixth Party doesn't marry, the party the Anti-Christ controls. Fallen angels would have only wanted sex with the human women, not marry them. The Protecting Angels looks and wisdom is how the 'sons of God' won the human women's hearts over to begin with. The angels were there to protect the human women, not to marry them. An Angelic Male is extremely handsome to a human woman and Angelic Female such as myself or Sheya, which is your 'Guardian Angel' is extremely gorgeous to a human man. The Protecting Angel for a man is a female and the Protecting Angel for a woman is a male angel. Remember when Rachael saw Sheya, your Protecting Angel for a second when Sheya was allowed to come into this vessel for a second to let Rachael see her and tell you what she looked like? When you asked about Sheya saying 'SSSsssshhhhhh' all the time to keep reminding you to settle down? Rachael said, 'WOW, She's gorgeous Walters.' Even to a human woman, an Angelic Female is gorgeous. There would be no competition. That's why God didn't want the species to intermix, that's also one of the reasons why God doesn't allow the humans to see Angelic Beings. He knew if the humans saw the Angelic Beings they would want to mate with them and not their own kind, which is an abomination. Lillith, being an Unclean Spirit now, would change her shape to whatever you wanted. She knows if she manifested herself to you the way she is, you wouldn't want anything to do with her. Lillith's true form now is a snake."

I asked, "Speaking of Sodom and Gomorrah, can a gay, lesbian, or transsexual be a Christian?" Lay Lay said, "No, a gay, lesbian, bi-sexual, transvestite, or transsexual is not a Christian. God put His foot down and destroyed Sodom, Gomorrah and other cities because of those abominations. I won't bother you with the names of the other cites, you wouldn't recognize them. Those characteristics are the characteristics of Lillith (The female) and Syenson (The male) 'unclean spirits'. As I said, God made women to be with men. God also made the sex of each at the split second of conception for that particular individual. What sex the individual human is, is determined by the soul and spirit that comes into the baby at the 'split second' of conception, when the sperm goes into the egg. Having a sex change is not the Will of the Father in Heaven for anyone. He created them the way they are supposed to live without changing their sex or sexual preference, no one is born that way. The sex of the soul and spirit is still the same sex the vessel was born as, no matter what the outside of the vessel looks like. What it is, is demonic possession (Unclean Spirits living in the human heart, soul, and spirit.), demonic obsession (The mind having an unreasonable idea or feeling.), or demonic oppression (Things outside the vessel, the vessel can't control like the laws of the land, culture, actions of other people that causes depression.). Any way you look at it, it's all demonic." I asked, "How can the vessel say the name of Jesus and be possessed?" Lay Lay said, "The vessel isn't actually saying which Jesus they are talking to or about. The Word of God says the demons will 'shudder at the name of Jesus Christ of Nazareth, not the name of Jesus. They can all say Jesus as long as they are not referring to Jesus Christ of Nazareth. Christians need to remember there are two different Jesus'. Christians also need to remember that the name of Jesus is not what defeated Satan. What defeated Satan was the Crucifixion, Blood, and Resurrection of Jesus Christ of Nazareth. Christians need to say the whole name of Jesus Christ of Nazareth and 'Plead the Blood' more which includes using the whole name of Jesus Christ of Nazareth. (Pleading the Blood in found at the end of the chapter called 'The Chat Room' in my book MATTHEW'S WORD 'TWO':REAL WORD OF GOD BIBLE.)

Genesis 19:5-8 (KJV)
5) And they called unto Lot, and said unto him, Where are the men which came in to thee this night? Bring them out unto us, that we may **know** them. (Knowing them, the men and women of the city were talking about having sex with the men, not inviting them in for tea and coffee.)
6) And Lot went out at the door unto them, and shut the door after him.
7) And said, I pray you, bretheren, **do not so wickedly.**
8) Behold (Getting the men and women's attention.), now, I have two daughters which have **not known** man; (Virgin daughters.) let me, I pray you, bring them out unto you, and do ye to them as is good in your eyes: only unto these men do nothing; for therefore came they under the shadow of my roof.

2 Corinthians 11:4 (KJV)
4) For if he that cometh preacheth **another Jesus**, whom we have not preached, or if ye receive another spirit, which ye have not received, or

another gospel, which ye have not accepted, ye might well bear with *him*. (The other Jesus is 180% opposite Jesus Christ of Nazareth.)

Leviticus 18:22) (KJV) Thou shalt not lie with mankind, as with womankind (Man is not to have sex with or make love to man and woman is not to have sex with or make love to woman): it *is* abomination."

Jude 1 (KJV)
5) I will therefore put you in remembrance, though ye once knew this, how that the Lord, having saved the people out of the land of Egypt, afterward destroyed them that believed not.
6) And the angels which kept not their first estate, but left their own habitation, he hath reserved in everlasting chains under darkness unto the judgment of the great day.
7) Even as Sodom and Gomorrah, and the cities about them in like manner, giving themselves over to fornication, and going after strange flesh, are set forth for an example, **suffering the VENGEANCE OF ETERNAL FIRE**."

       Lay Lay continued, "Let me break this down into human terms so you can understand it. There is a difference between Fleshly Desire Sin which is drinking, smoking, swearing, lust, etc., which are 'masks to cover up for the pain in the heart. These are all Learned Sins of the flesh. Lust is a little different because you don't actually have to do anything with the human in the flesh, just the mind which is connected to the heart. It's still a fleshly desire, just thinking about having sex with a man or woman is adultery or fornication because the lust goes to your heart. The vessel 'learning' the characteristics of the unclean spirit. So far it's the healing of the heart that's needed, not deliverance. Once the heart is healed from the pain and anguish the vessel will usually stop the sinning on its own given enough time. Just like Detta is Anorexic, it will stop on it's own once she gets used to getting some control in her life. The demons are in the vessel for an Unclean Spirit Sin. Where Christians get confused is when a Fleshly Desire Sin becomes an Unclean Spirit Sin. Being with a man is spiritually built into a woman, but being with a man for an independent woman would mean the woman would have to give up her independence. That's why she won't submit all of her heart to Jesus and Jesus won't accept a half-hearted prayer, like Tony. A man/woman with a low self-image just wants someone in his/her life to accept him/her, love him/her, care for him/her. The 'unclean spirits' get the man and man or woman and woman to have sex with each other and then attaches itself or enters the vessels with his friends. Humans have heard ministers say many times behind the pulpit, 'Come as you are, Jesus will accept you as you are'. They come and say a half-hearted prayer of salvation, meaning they will accept Jesus if He allows them to keep their sexual preferences and their old lifestyle. They expect Jesus to allow them to continue their life-style and Jesus won't allow that. Jesus will accept them as they are, but the condition is that they allow Jesus changes their way of living and life style to His characteristics. The vessel wants to be left with the characteristics of Satan." Therefore, their Sinners Prayer is in vain, Jesus Christ of Nazareth doesn't accept it." I asked, "Then why do a lot of gays and lesbians believe they are saved?" Lay Lay said, "Because of Religious Unclean Spirits."

JACOB

AND

JOSEPH

(CONTINUED FROM: HEAVENLY ANGEL LAY LAY EXPLAINS BIBLE TO READ, WHICH BIBLE NOT TO READ, AND WHY)

JOSEPH

GENESIS 43:1-34

1) And the famine was sore (really bad) in the land.

2) And it came to pass, when they had eaten up the corn which they had brought out of Egypt, their father said unto them, Go again, buy us a little food.

3) And Judah spake unto him, saying, The man (Joseph) did solemnly protest unto (warn) us, saying, Ye shall not see my face (do not come to me again), except your brother (Benjamin) be with you.

4) If thou wilt (you will) send our brother (Benjamin) with us, we will go down and buy thee (you) food:

5) But if thou wilt (you will) not send him (Benjamin), we will not go down: for the man (Joseph) said unto us, Ye shall not see my face, except your brother (Benjamin) be with you.

6) And Israel said, Wherefore dealt ye so ill with me, as to tell the man (Joseph) whether ye had yet a brother?

7) And they said, The man (Joseph) asked us straitly of our state, and of our kindred, saying, Is your father yet alive? have ye another brother? and we told him according to the tenor of these words: could we certainly know that he would say, Bring your brother down?

8) And Judah said unto Israel his father, Send the lad with me, and we will arise and go; that we may live, and not die, both we, and thou, and also our little ones (children).

9) I will be surety for him (Benjamin); of my hand shalt thou require him: if I bring him not unto thee, and set him before thee, then let

me bear the blame for ever: (if Judah doesn't bring Benjamin back to Jacob, Judah will bear the blame forever)

10) For except we had lingered, surely now we had returned this second time.

11) And their father Israel said unto them, If it must be so now, do this; take of the best fruits in the land in your vessels, and carry down the man (Joseph) a present, a little balm, and a little honey, spices, and myrrh, nuts, and almonds:

12) And take double money in your hand; and the money that was brought again in the mouth of your sacks, carry it again in your hand; peradventure (perhaps) it was an oversight:

13) Take also your brother (Benjamin), and arise, go again unto the man (Joseph):

14) And God Almighty give you mercy before the man, that he may send away your other brother (Simeon), and Benjamin. If I be bereaved of my children, I am bereaved.

15) And the men took that present, and they took double money in their hand and Benjamin; and rose up, and went down to Egypt, and stood before Joseph.

16) And when Joseph saw Benjamin with them, he said to the ruler of his house, Bring these men home, and slay, and make ready; for these men shall dine with me at noon.

17) And the man did as Joseph bade (said); and the man brought the men into Joseph's house.

18) And the men were afraid, because they were brought into Joseph's house; and they said, Because of the money that was returned in our sacks at the first time are we brought in; that he may seek occasion against us, and fall upon us, and take us for bondmen, and our asses.

19) And they came near to the steward of Joseph's house, and they communed with (talked with) him (the ruler of Joseph's house) at the door of the house,

20) And said, O sir, we came indeed down at the first time to buy food:

21) And it came to pass, when we came to the inn, that we opened our sacks, and, behold, every man's money was in the mouth of his sack, our money in full weight: and we have brought it again in our

hand.

22) And other money have we brought down in our hands to buy food: we cannot tell who put our money in our sacks.

23) And he (the ruler of Joseph's house) said, Peace be to you, fear not: your God, and the God of your father, hath given you treasure in your sacks: I had your money. And he (the ruler of Joseph's house) brought Simeon out unto them.

24) And the man (the ruler of Joseph's house) brought the men (the brothers) into Joseph's house, and gave them (the brothers) water, and they (the brothers) washed their feet; and he (the ruler of Joseph's house) gave their asses provender (food).

25) And they (the brothers) made ready the present against Joseph came at noon: for they heard that they should eat bread there.

26) And when Joseph came home, they brought him the present which was in their hand into the house, and bowed themselves to him to the earth. (the dream Joseph had is coming to past. The brothers are bowing down to Joseph)

27) And he (Joseph) asked them (the brothers) of their welfare, and said, Is your father well, the old man of whom ye spake? Is he yet alive?

28) And they (the brothers) answered, Thy (your) servant our father is in good health, he is yet alive. And they bowed down their heads, and made obeisance.

29) And he (Joseph) lifted up his eyes, and saw his brother Benjamin, his mother's son, and said, Is this your younger brother, of whom ye spake unto me? And he said, God be gracious unto thee, my son.

30) And Joseph made haste; for his bowels did yearn upon his brother: and he sought where to weep; and he entered into his chamber, and wept there.

31) And he (Joseph) washed his face, and went out, and refrained himself, and said, Set on bread.

32) And they set on for him by himself, and for them by themselves, and for the Egyptians, which did eat with him, by themselves: because the Egyptians might not eat bread with the Hebrews; for that is an abomination unto the Egyptians.

33) And they (the brothers) sat before him (Joseph), the firstborn

according to his birthright, and the youngest according to his youth: and the men marvelled one at another.

34) And he (Joseph) took and sent messes (the quantity of food, or serving) unto them (the brothers) from before him (Joseph): but Benjamin's mess (serving) was five times so much as any of their's. And they (the brothers) drank, and were merry with him (Joseph).

GENESIS 44:1-34

1) And he (Joseph) commanded the steward of his house, saying, Fill the men's (Joseph's brothers) sacks with food, as much as they can carry, and put every man's money in his sack's mouth.

2) And put my cup, the silver cup, in the sack's mouth of the youngest, and his corn money. And he (the steward of Joseph's house) did according to the word that Joseph had spoken.

3) As soon as the morning was light, the men (the brothers) were sent away, they and their asses.

4) And when they (the brothers) were gone out of the city, and not yet far off, Joseph said unto his steward, Up, follow after the men; and when thou dost overtake them, say unto them, Wherefore have ye rewarded evil for good?

5) Is not this it in which my lord drinketh, and whereby indeed he divineth? ye have done evil in so doing.

6) And he (the steward) overtook them (Joseph's brothers), and he (the steward) spake (spoke) unto them (Joseph's brothers) these same words.

7) And they (Joseph's brothers) said unto him (the steward of Joseph's house), Wherefore saith my lord these words? God forbid that thy servants should do according to this thing:

8) Behold (remember), the money, which we found in our sacks' mouths, we brought again unto thee (you) out of the land of Canaan: how then should we steal out of thy (your) lord's house silver or gold?

9) With whomsoever of thy servants it be found, both let him die, and we also will be my lord's bondmen. (Doesn't this remind you of Jacob saying those words before he knew Rachel had stolen the 'idols' that Laban, Rachel's father, worshipped?)

10) And he (the steward of Joseph's house) said, Now also let it be

according unto your words: he with whom it is found (Joseph's cup) shall be my servant; and ye (you) shall be blameless.

11) Then they (Joseph's brothers) speedily took down every man his sack to the ground, and opened every man his sack.

12) And he (the steward of Joseph's house) searched, and began at the eldest, and left at the youngest: and the cup was found in Benjamin's sack.

13) Then they (Joseph's brothers) rent (tore) their clothes, and laded every man his ass, and returned to the city.

14) And Judah (Remember, Judah was the brother who sold Joseph to the Ishmeelites to begin with, married a Canaanite woman, and had sex with Tamar, his daughter in law who was posing as a 'whore', after Judah didn't keep his promise to Tamar to wed Judah's youngest son, Shelah when Shelah was of age for marriage, and Tamar conceived Judah's child) and his brethren came to Joseph's house; for he was yet there: and they fell before him (Joseph) on the ground.

15) And Joseph said unto them, What deed is this that ye have done? wot ye not that such a man as I can certainly divine?

16) And Judah said, What shall we say unto my lord? what shall we speak? or how shall we clear ourselves? God hath found out the iniquity of thy (your) servants: behold, we are my lord's servants, both we, and he also with whom the cup is found.

17) And he (Joseph) said, God forbid that I should do so: but the man in whose hand the cup is found, he shall be my servant; and as for you, get you up in peace unto your father.

18) Then Judah came near unto him, and said, Oh my lord, let thy (your) servant, I pray thee, speak a word in my lord's ears, and let not thine (your) **anger** burn against thy (your) servant: for thou art even as Pharaoh. (**I underlined <u>Anger</u> here because I wanted to bring it to your attention that even Joseph got angry. Judah knew even a human in a high place could get angry, it's human to get angry, that's the way human's are made, with emotions, and anger is an emotion, just like Heavenly Angel Lay Lay said**)

19) My lord asked his servants, saying, Have ye a father, or a brother?

20) And we said unto my lord, We have a father, an old man, and a

child of his old age, a little one; and his brother is dead, and he alone (the child) is left of his mother, and his father loveth him (now we know by the term 'a child' that Benjamin is not that old.

21) And thou saidst unto thy servants, Bring him down unto me, that I may set mine eyes upon him.

22) And we said unto my lord, The lad (now we know Benjamin is probably in his pre-teen to early teen years. Certainly not old enough to take care of himself or travel alone) cannot leave his father: for if he should leave his father, his father would die.

23) And thou saidst unto thy servants (you said to us), Except your youngest brother (Benjamin) come down (journey to Egypt) with you, ye shall see my face no more.

24) And it came to pass when we came up unto thy servant my father, we told him the words of my lord.

25) And our father said, Go again, and buy us a little food.

26) And we said, We cannot go down: if our youngest brother be with us, then will we go down: for we may not see the man's face, except our youngest brother be with us.

27) And thy (your) servant my father said unto us, Ye (you) know that my wife (Rachel) bare me (Isaac) two sons (the only two sons that Rachel did bear to Isaac was Joseph in Haran and Benjamin in Canaan. Rachel died during the child birth of Benjamin):

28) And the one (Joseph) went out from me, and I said, Surely he (Joseph) is torn in pieces; and I saw him not since (Jacob hadn't seen Joseph since):

29) And if ye (you) take this (Benjamin) also from me (Jacob), and mischief befall him (Benjamin), ye (you) shall bring down my gray hairs with sorrow to the grave.

30) Now therefore when I come to thy (your) servant my father, and the lad (Benjamin) be not with us; seeing that his life is bound up in the lad's life;

31) It shall come to pass, when he (Jacob) seeth that the lad is not with us, that he (Jacob) will die: and thy (your) servants shall bring down the gray hairs of thy (your) servant our father with sorrow to the grave.

32) For thy (your) servant became surety (somebody who assumes responsibility for another's obligations in case of default,

particularly by giving a guarantee) (Encarta ® World English Dictionary © & (P) 1998-2004 Microsoft Corporation. All rights reserved.) for the lad (Benjamin) unto my father, saying, If I bring him (Benjamin) not unto thee (Jacob), then I shall bear the blame to my father for ever.

33) Now therefore, I pray thee, let thy (your) servant (Judah) abide instead of the lad (Benjamin) a bondman to my lord; and let the lad (Benjamin) go up (back to Hebron, in Canaan) with his brethren.

34) For how shall I go up to my father, and the lad be not with me? lest peradventure I see the evil that shall come on my father.

GENESIS 45:1-28

1) **Then Joseph could not refrain himself before all them (the brothers) that stood by him; and he (Joseph) <u>cried,</u>** Cause every man to go out from me. And there stood no man with him, while Joseph made himself known unto his brethren.

2) **And he (Joseph) <u>wept aloud</u>:** and the Egyptians and the house of Pharaoh heard. (why did I make the last two scriptures bold and underline those specific words? Crying and weeping is 180 degrees opposite anger. Just like anything else like Heavenly Angle Lay Lay said, more about this in my book MATTHEW'S WORD 'TWO':REAL WORD OF GOD BIBLE) **So many women ask why men can't show their emotions. The reason is because when a man is punished in any way for showing his negative emotions such as getting angry with his girlfriend or wife, he hides all his emotions. Women can't have the men show their positive emotions and keep their negative emotions bottled up or sooner or later the negative emotion will surface. It's better to let the man show his negative emotion when the negative emotion has a reason to form and express itself instead of waiting until his human heart and mind can not contain any more negative emotions. The same with the positive emotions, women want the man to show their positive emotions right then, but if we have been scolded when we show our negative emotions we won't be so willing to show our positive emotions to anyone, including the woman we are close to)**

3) And Joseph said unto his brethren (brothers), I am Joseph; doth

my father (Jacob) yet live? And his (Joseph's) brethren could not answer him (Joseph); for they were troubled at his presence.

4) And Joseph said unto his brethren, Come near to me, I pray you. And they came near. And he said, I am Joseph your brother, whom ye sold into Egypt.

5) Now therefore be not grieved, nor angry with yourselves, that ye sold me hither (here): for God did send me before you to preserve life.

6) For these two years hath the famine been in the land: and yet there are five years, in the which there shall neither be earing (shipments of food in or out of Egypt) nor harvest.

7) And God sent me before you to preserve you a posterity in the earth, and to save your lives by a great deliverance.

8) So now it was not you that sent me hither, but God (God saw to the sale of Joseph to the Ishmeelites and the journey to Egypt. No matter how bad things may appear, 'All things work out for the good for those who love the Lord'): and he (God) hath made me a father to Pharaoh, and lord of all his house, and a ruler throughout all the land of Egypt.

9) Haste ye (go quickly), and go up to my father, and say unto him, Thus saith thy son Joseph, God hath made me lord of all Egypt: come down unto me, tarry not (don't wait):

10) And thou (you) shalt dwell (live) in the land of Goshen, and thou shalt be near unto me, thou, and thy children, and thy children's children, and thy flocks, and thy herds, and all that thou hast:

11) And there will I nourish thee; for yet there are five years of famine; lest thou, and thy household, and all that thou hast, come to poverty. (if you don't come to me, all you have and your households have will be lost)

12) And, behold, your eyes see, and the eyes of my brother Benjamin, that it is my mouth that speaketh unto you.

13) And ye shall tell my father of all my glory in Egypt, and of all that ye have seen; and ye shall haste (hurry) and bring down my father hither (to Egypt).

14) And he (Joseph) fell upon his brother Benjamin's neck, and wept; and Benjamin wept upon his (Joseph's) neck.

15) Moreover he (Joseph) kissed all his brethren, and wept upon

them: and after that his brethren talked with him (Joseph).

16) And the fame thereof was heard in Pharaoh's house, saying, Joseph's brethren are come: and it pleased Pharaoh well, and his servants.

17) And Pharaoh said unto Joseph, Say unto thy (your) brethren, This do ye (you); lade (load) your beasts, and go, get you unto the land of Canaan;

18) And take your father (Jacob) and your households (relatives), and come unto me: and I will give you the good of the land of Egypt, and ye (you) shall eat the fat of the land. (the good of the crops of Egypt)

19) Now thou art commanded, this do ye; take you wagons out of the land of Egypt for your little ones, and for your wives, and bring your father, and come. (take the wagons and load the wagons with your children and wives and bring Jacob with them to Egypt)

20) Also regard not your stuff (leave everything you have); for the good of all the land of Egypt is your's. (Egypt will replace all your goods)

21) And the children of Israel did so: and Joseph gave them wagons, according to the commandment of Pharaoh, and gave them provision (food) for the way.

22) To all of them (his brothers) he (Joseph) gave each man changes of raiment; but to Benjamin he (Joseph) gave three hundred pieces of silver, and five changes of raiment.

23) And to his father (Jacob) he (Joseph) sent after this manner; ten asses laden (loaded) with the good things of Egypt, and ten she asses laden with corn and bread and meat for his father by the way.

24) So he (Joseph) sent his brethren away, and they (Joseph's brothers) departed: and he (Joseph) said unto them (his brothers) , See that ye (you) fall not out by the way.

25) And they (Joseph's brothers) went up out of Egypt, and came into the land of Canaan unto Jacob their father,

26) And told him (Jacob), saying, Joseph is yet alive, and he (Joseph) is governor over all the land of Egypt. And Jacob's heart fainted, for he believed them not. (Jacob didn't believe his sons)

27) And they (Jacob's sons) told him (Jacob) all the words of Joseph, which he had said unto them: and when he (Jacob) saw the

wagons which Joseph had sent to carry him, the spirit of Jacob their father revived:

28) And Israel (Remember now, Jacob and Israel are the same man, Jacob's name was changed to Israel when Jacob wrestled with the angle all night and won. That story is often told as 'Jacob's Ladder'. Israel must have been a big man. I remember when Protecting Angel Shadow faced the Anti-Christ and Shadow had to look up to the Anti-Christ. More about this topic in my book MATTHEW'S WORD 'TWO':REAL WORD OF GOD BIBLE. Men back then had to have been bigger and taller than any man is today) said, It is enough; Joseph my son is yet alive: I will go and see him before I die.

GENESIS 46:1-34

1) And Israel took his journey with all that he had, and came to Beersheba, and offered sacrifices unto the God of his father Isaac. (Jacob traveled from Hebron to Beersheba about 40 miles or 66.8 kilometers south west. 40 miles/25 miles or 41.75 kilometers per day travel=1.6 days travel)

2) And God spake unto Israel in the visions of the night, and said, Jacob, Jacob. And he said, Here am I.

3) And he said, I am God, the God of thy father: fear not to go down into Egypt; for I will there make of thee a great nation:

4) I will go down with thee into Egypt; and I will also surely bring thee up again: and Joseph shall put his hand upon thine eyes.

5) And Jacob rose up from Beersheba: and the sons of Israel carried Jacob their father, and their little ones, and their wives, in the wagons which Pharaoh had sent to carry him.

6) And they (all the descendants of Jacob) took their cattle, and their goods, which they had gotten in the land of Canaan, and came into Egypt, Jacob, and all his seed (children, grandchildren, etc) with him:

7) His sons, and his sons' sons with him, his daughters, and his sons' daughters, and all his seed brought he with him into Egypt.

8) And these are the names of the children of Israel, which came into Egypt, Jacob and his sons: Reuben, Jacob's firstborn.

9) And the sons of Reuben; Hanoch, and Phallu, and Hezron, and

Carmi.

10) And the sons of Simeon; Jemuel, and Jamin, and Ohad, and Jachin, and Zohar, and Shaul the son of a Canaanitish woman.

11) And the sons of Levi; Gershon, Kohath, and Merari.

12) And the sons of Judah; Er, and Onan, and Shelah, and Pharez, and Zarah: but Er and Onan died in the land of Canaan. And the sons of Pharez were Hezron and Hamul.

13) And the sons of Issachar; Tola, and Phuvah, and Job, and Shimron.

14) And the sons of Zebulun; Sered, and Elon, and Jahleel.

15) These be the sons of Leah, which she bare unto Jacob in Padanaram, with his daughter Dinah: all the souls of his sons and his daughters were thirty and three.

16) And the sons of Gad; Ziphion, and Haggi, Shuni, and Ezbon, Eri, and Arodi, and Areli.

17) And the sons of Asher; Jimnah, and Ishuah, and Isui, and Beriah, and Serah their sister: and the sons of Beriah; Heber, and Malchiel.

18) These are the sons of Zilpah, whom Laban gave to Leah his daughter, and these she bare unto Jacob, even sixteen souls.

19) The sons of Rachel Jacob's wife; Joseph, and Benjamin.

20) And unto Joseph in the land of Egypt were born Manasseh and Ephraim, which Asenath the daughter of Potipherah priest of On bare unto him.

21) And the sons of Benjamin were Belah, and Becher, and Ashbel, Gera, and Naaman, Ehi, and Rosh, Muppim, and Huppim, and Ard.

22) These are the sons of Rachel, which were born to Jacob: all the souls were fourteen.

23) And the sons of Dan; Hushim.

24) And the sons of Naphtali; Jahzeel, and Guni, and Jezer, and Shillem.

25) These are the sons of Bilhah, which Laban gave unto Rachel his daughter, and she bare these unto Jacob: all the souls were seven.

26) All the souls that came with Jacob into Egypt, which came out of his loins, besides Jacob's sons' wives, all the souls were threescore and six;

27) And the sons of Joseph, which were born him in Egypt, were

two souls: all the souls of the house of Jacob, which came into Egypt, were threescore and ten.

28) And he (Jacob) sent Judah before him (Jacob) unto Joseph, to direct his face unto Goshen; and they (all the descendants of Jacob) came into the land of Goshen.

29) And Joseph made ready his chariot, and went up to meet Israel his father, to Goshen, and presented himself (Joseph) unto him (Jacob); and he (Jacob) fell on his (Joseph's) neck, and wept on his (Joseph's) neck a good while.

30) And Israel said unto Joseph, Now let me die, since I have seen thy face, because thou art (Joseph is) yet alive.

31) And Joseph said unto his brethren, and unto his father's house, I will go up, and shew Pharaoh, and say unto him, My brethren, and my father's house, which were in the land of Canaan, are come unto me;

32) And the men are shepherds, for their trade hath been to feed cattle; and they have brought their flocks, and their herds, and all that they have.

33) And it shall come to pass, when Pharaoh shall call you, and shall say, What is your occupation?

34) That ye shall say, Thy servants' trade hath been about cattle from our youth even until now, both we, and also our fathers: that ye may dwell in the land of Goshen; for every shepherd is an abomination unto the Egyptians. (Beersheba to Goshen is unknown. There really isn't any factual knowledge about where Goshen was that I have been able to find. The theorists assume Goshen was on the Northern boundary of Egypt, so for this book we will use the City of On, Egypt for any calculations of travel in miles and kilometers. If anyone is wondering why I use miles and kilometers, it's because these books go World Wide. Even though the United States is still using miles, there are a lot of countries who already use kilometers. Beersheba to Kadesh-Barnea is 55 miles or 91.85 kilometers south west. Kadesh-Barnea to On, Egypt is 175 miles or 292.25 kilometers south. 55+175=230 miles or 91.85+292.25=384.10 kilometers south. 230/25 miles per day=9.2 days/6 days per week=1.6 weeks. 384.10 kilometers/41.75 kilometers per day=9.2 days/6 days per week=1.6 weeks)

GENESIS 47:1-31

1) Then Joseph came and told Pharaoh, and said, My father and my brethren, and their flocks, and their herds, and all that they have, are come out of the land of Canaan; and, behold, they are in the land of Goshen.

2) And he (Joseph) took some of his (Joseph's) brethren, even five men, and presented them (Joseph's brothers) unto Pharaoh.

3) And Pharaoh said unto his brethren, What is your occupation? And they said unto Pharaoh, Thy (your) servants are shepherds, both we, and also our fathers.

4) They (Joseph's brothers) said morever (continued saying) unto Pharaoh, For to sojourn (temporarily live) in the land are we come; for thy (your) servants have no pasture for their flocks; for the famine is sore in the land of Canaan: now therefore, we pray thee (they are asking the Pharaoh), let thy (your) servants dwell in the land of Goshen.

5) And Pharaoh spake unto Joseph, saying, Thy father and thy brethren are come unto thee (you):

6) The land of Egypt is before thee you); in the best of the land make thy (your) father and brethren to dwell (live); in the land of Goshen let them dwell: and if thou knowest any men of activity among them, then make them rulers over my cattle.

7) And Joseph brought in Jacob his father, and set him before Pharaoh: and Jacob blessed Pharaoh.

8) And Pharaoh said unto Jacob, How old art thou?

9) And **Jacob** said unto Pharaoh, The days of the years of my pilgrimage are **an hundred and thirty years**: <u>few and evil have the days of the years of my life been, and have not attained unto the days of the years of the life of my fathers in the days of their pilgrimage</u>. (Evil causes stress and stress shortens the life of humans)

10) And Jacob blessed Pharaoh, and went out from before Pharaoh.

11) And Joseph placed his father and his brethren, and gave them a possession in the land of Egypt, in the best of the land, in the land of Rameses, as Pharaoh had commanded.

12) And Joseph nourished his father, and his brethren, and all his

father's household, with bread, according to their families.

13) And there was no bread in all the land; for the famine was very sore, so that the land of Egypt and all the land of Canaan fainted by reason of the famine.

14) And Joseph gathered up all the money that was found in the land of Egypt, and in the land of Canaan, for the corn which they (the people) bought: and Joseph brought the money into Pharaoh's house. (All the money was Pharaoh's, people didn't have any more money)

15) And when money failed in the land of Egypt, and in the land of Canaan, all the Egyptians came unto Joseph, and said, Give us bread: for why should we die in thy presence? for the money faileth.

16) And Joseph said, Give your cattle; and I will give you for your cattle, if money fail. (If the people were broke, Joseph would take their cattle in exchange for food)

17) And they brought their cattle unto Joseph: and Joseph gave them bread in exchange for horses, and for the flocks, and for the cattle of the herds, and for the asses: and he (Joseph) fed them (the people) with bread for all their cattle for that year.

18) When that year was ended, they (the people) came unto him (Joseph) the second year, and said unto him (Joseph), We will not hide it from my lord, how that our money is spent; my lord also hath our herds of cattle; there is not ought left in the sight of my lord, but our bodies, and our lands: (All the people had left was their land and their lives)

19) Wherefore shall we die before thine (your) eyes, both we and our land? buy us and our land for bread, and we and our land will be servants unto Pharaoh: and give us seed, that we may live, and not die, that the land be not desolate. (the people are selling themselves into slavery)

20) And Joseph bought all the land of Egypt for Pharaoh; for the Egyptians sold every man his field, because the famine prevailed over them: so the land became Pharaoh's.

21) And as for the people, he removed them to cities from one end of the borders of Egypt even to the other end thereof.

22) Only the land of the priests bought he not; for the priests had a

portion assigned them of Pharaoh, and did eat their portion which Pharaoh gave them: wherefore they sold not their lands. (the only land Pharaoh did not own was the land of the priests)

23) Then Joseph said unto the people, Behold, I have bought you this day and your land for Pharaoh: lo, here is seed for you, and ye shall sow the land. (now the people are growing crops on the fields that used to belong to them for Pharaoh)

24) And it shall come to pass in the increase, that ye shall give the fifth part unto Pharaoh, and four parts shall be your own, for seed of the field, and for your food, and for them of your households, and for food for your little ones. (they have to pay Pharaoh twice the amount God wants for tithes. The average family in the United States pays more than a fifth, we pay one third in taxes. The other four fifths is theirs for living, reseeding, eating, etc. The average family in the United States gets two thirds, only half the amount they had to live on)

25) And they said, Thou hast saved our lives: let us find grace in the sight of my lord, and we will be Pharaoh's servants.

26) And Joseph made it a law over the land of Egypt unto this day, that Pharaoh should have the fifth part, except the land of the priests only, which became not Pharaoh's. (Pharaoh was to get the fifth part, the last part, not the first fifth, but the last fifth part. In others words, if there wasn't quite enough to go around, Pharaoh received the smaller fifth, not the regular fifth)

27) And Israel dwelt in the land of Egypt, in the country of Goshen; and they had possessions therein, and grew, and multiplied exceedingly.

28) And **Jacob lived in the land of Egypt seventeen years**: so the whole age of **Jacob was an hundred forty and seven years**.

29) And the time drew nigh that Israel must die (Jacob is about to die): and he (Jacob) called his son Joseph, and said unto him (Joseph), If now I have found grace in thy sight, put, I pray thee, thy hand under my thigh, and deal kindly and truly with me; bury me not, I pray thee, in Egypt:

30) But I will lie with my fathers, and thou shalt carry me out of Egypt, and bury me in their buryingplace. And he (Joseph) said, I will do as thou (you) hast said.

31) And he (Jacob) said, Swear unto me. And he (Joseph) sware unto him (Jacob). And Israel bowed himself upon the bed's head.

GENESIS 48:1-22

1) And it came to pass after these things, that one (a servant) told Joseph, Behold, thy (your) father is sick: and he (Joseph) took with him his two sons, Manasseh and Ephraim.

2) And one (a servant) told Jacob, and said, Behold, thy son Joseph cometh unto thee (you): and Israel strengthened himself, and sat upon the bed. (struggled to sit up on his bed)

3) And Jacob said unto Joseph, God Almighty appeared unto me at Luz in the land of Canaan, and blessed me,

4) And said unto me, Behold, I will make thee (you) fruitful, and multiply thee (you), and I will make of thee a multitude of people; and will give this land to thy (your) seed after thee (you) for an everlasting possession.

5) And now thy (your) two sons, Ephraim and Manasseh, which were born unto thee (you) in the land of Egypt before I came unto thee (you) into Egypt, are mine; as Reuben and Simeon, they shall be mine.

6) And thy issue, which thou begettest after them, shall be thine, and shall be called after the name of their brethren in their inheritance. (in other words, all that Jacob has including Reuben and Simeon are to be Joseph's after Jacob dies. Like a Jacob's 'Last Will and Testament' in terms of the United States)

7) And as for me (Jacob), when I came from Padan, Rachel died by me (Jacob) in the land of Canaan in the way, when yet there was but a little way to come unto Ephrath: and I buried her (Rachel) there in the way of Ephrath; the same is Bethlehem.

8) And Israel beheld Joseph's sons, and said, Who are these? (asking about Joseph's sons. Jacob couldn't see.)

9) And Joseph said unto his father, They are my sons, whom God hath given me in this place. And he (Jacob) said, Bring them, I pray thee, unto me, and I will bless them (your sons).

10) Now the eyes of Israel were dim for age, so that he (Jacob) could not see. And he (Joseph) brought them (Joseph's sons) near unto him (Jacob); and he (Jacob) kissed them (Joseph's sons), and

embraced them (Joseph's sons).

11) And Israel said unto Joseph, I had not thought to see thy face (Jacob didn't think he would ever see Joseph again): and, lo, God hath shewed me also thy seed (and God has not only let Jacob see Joseph again, but also Joseph's children).

12) And Joseph brought them (his sons) out from between his (Jacob's) knees, and he (Joseph) bowed himself with his face to the earth.

13) And Joseph took them both, Ephraim in his right hand toward Israel's left hand, and Manasseh in his left hand toward Israel's right hand, and brought them (the children) near unto him (Jacob).

14) And Israel stretched out his right hand, and laid it upon Ephraim's head, who was the younger, and his left hand upon Manasseh's head, guiding his hands wittingly; for Manasseh was the firstborn.

15) And he (Jacob) blessed Joseph, and said, God, before whom my fathers Abraham and Isaac did walk, the God which fed me all my life long unto this day,

16) The Angel which redeemed me from all evil, bless the lads; and let my name be named on them, and the name of my fathers Abraham and Isaac; and let them grow into a multitude in the midst of the earth.

17) And when Joseph saw that his father laid his right hand upon the head of Ephraim (the younger), it displeased him (Joseph): and he (Joseph) held up his father's (Jacob's) hand, to remove it from Ephraim's head unto Manasseh's head.

18) And Joseph said unto his father, Not so, my father: for this is the firstborn; put thy right hand upon his head.

19) And his father (Jacob) refused, and said, I know it, my son, I know it: he (the first born, Manasseh) also shall become a people (nation), and he (Manasseh) also shall be great: but truly his younger brother (Ephraim) shall be greater than he (Manasseh), and his seed (Ephraim's children) shall become a multitude of nations.

20) And he (Jacob) blessed them (Manasseh and Ephraim) that day, saying, In thee (you) shall Israel bless, saying, God make thee (you) as Ephraim and as Manasseh: and he set Ephraim before Manasseh.

21) And Israel said unto Joseph, Behold, I die: but God shall be

with you, and bring you again unto the land of your fathers (you will return to Hebron in Canaan).

22) Moreover I have given to thee (you) one portion above thy brethren (your brothers), which I took out of the hand of the Amorite with my sword and with my bow.

GENESIS 49:1-33

1) And Jacob called unto his sons, and said, Gather yourselves together, that I may tell you that which shall befall you in the last days (Jacob is starting a Prophesy, the future events).

2) Gather yourselves together, and hear, ye sons of Jacob; and hearken unto (listen to) Israel your father.

3) Reuben, thou art my firstborn, my might, and the beginning of my strength, the excellency of dignity, and the excellency of power:

4) Unstable as water, thou shalt not excel; because thou wentest up to thy father's bed; then defiledst thou it: he went up to my couch.

     Genesis 35:21-22

     21) And Israel journeyed, and spread his tent beyond the tower of Edar.

     22) And it came to pass, when Israel dwelt in that land, that Reuben went and lay with Bilhah his father's concubine: and Israel heard it. Now the sons of Jacob were twelve:

5) Simeon and Levi are brethren; instruments of cruelty are in their habitations.

6) O my soul, come not thou into their secret; unto their assembly, mine honour, be not thou united: for in their anger they slew a man, and in their selfwill they digged down a wall.

     Genesis 34:1-31

     1) And Dinah the daughter of Leah, which she (Leah) bare unto Jacob, went out to see the daughters of the land.

     2) And when Shechem the son of Hamor the Hivite, prince of the country, saw her, he took her, and lay with her, and defiled (deprive woman of virginity: to be the first man to have sexual intercourse with a woman, usually outside marriage) (Encarta ® World English Dictionary © & (P) 1998-2004 Microsoft Corporation. All rights reserved.) her. (I've heard that Shechem

raped Dinah, but he didn't there is no indication of a rape, taking Dinah without her consent. The way the scriptures that follow are reading, Shechem and Dinah both were willing to go all the way with each other. If there had been a rape, the talk wouldn't have been for Shechem to marry Dinah, nor would the scripture say Shechem, the Prince of Shalem, love Dinah and speaking kindly of Dinah.)

3) And his soul clave unto Dinah the daughter of Jacob, and he loved the damsel, and spake kindly unto the damsel.

4) And Shechem spake unto his father Hamor, saying, Get me this damsel to wife. (Shechem, the prince of Shalem, wants to marry Dinah. That would make Dinah a princess. When a boy says that to his father and the father is the king of a country, that boy could have any pick of women in that country. Dinah would be a princess over all the land, and eventually the queen of the land. Does that sound like Rape? Not to me it doesn't. It sounds like they started flirting with each other, kissing, petting and things went too far, but they were both consensual in the act)

5) And Jacob heard that he (Shechem, the prince of Shalem) had defiled (deprive woman of virginity: to be the first man to have sexual intercourse with a woman, usually outside marriage) (Encarta ® World English Dictionary © & (P) 1998-2004 Microsoft Corporation. All rights reserved.) Dinah his (Jacob's) daughter: now his sons were with his cattle in the field: and Jacob held his peace until they were come.

6) And Hamor the father of Shechem went out unto Jacob to commune (talk) with him (Jacob).

7) And the sons of Jacob came out of the field when they heard it: and the men were grieved, and they were very wroth (angry) (See, there are all kinds of people in the Old Testament who got angry just like Heavenly Angel Lay Lay said there were. It's not wrong to get angry like a lot of secular or Christian counselors say or teach, what is wrong is allowing that anger to go to the extreme. What is an extreme? Using more anger and force than necessary to get the job done when the job could have been done with less force. How can you tell? Each situation and group of people or couples in a marriage or relationship is different. If the extreme is used once,

next time don't use as much. Learn to not only listen, but hear and communicate. Getting angry is actually human, anger is a human emotion), because he (Shechem) had wrought folly (a thoughtless or reckless behavior) in Israel in lying with Jacob's daughter: which thing ought not to be done.

8) And Hamor communed with them (Jacob and Dinah's brothers), saying, The soul of my son Shechem longeth for your daughter: I pray you give her (Dinah) him to wife. (The King of Shalem wants Jacob to give Dinah to Shechem, his son, the Prince of Shalem to be Shechem's wife)

9) And make ye marriages with us, and give your daughters unto us, and take our daughters unto you. (Intercultural marriages)

10) And ye shall dwell with us: and the land shall be before you; dwell and trade ye therein, and get you possessions therein.

11) And Shechem said unto her father and unto her brethren, Let me find grace in your eyes, and what ye shall say unto me I will give.

12) Ask me never so much dowry and gift, and I will give according as ye shall say unto me: but give me the damsel to wife.

13) And the sons of Jacob answered Shechem and Hamor his father deceitfully, and said, because he had defiled Dinah their sister:

14) And they said unto them, We cannot do this thing, to give our sister to one that is uncircumcised; for that were a reproach unto us:

15) But in this will we consent unto you: If ye will be as we be, that every male of you be circumcised;

16) Then will we give our daughters unto you, and we will take your daughters to us, and we will dwell with you, and we will become one people.

17) But if ye will not hearken unto us, to be circumcised; then will we take our daughter, and we will be gone.

18) And their words pleased Hamor, and Shechem Hamor's son.

19) And the young man deferred not to do the thing, because he had delight in Jacob's daughter: and he was more honourable than all the house of his father.

20) And Hamor and Shechem his son came into the gate of their city, and communed with the men of their city, saying,

21) These men are peaceable with us; therefore let them dwell in the land, and trade therein; for the land, behold, it is large enough for them; let us take their daughters to us for wives, and let us give them our daughters.

22) Only herein will the men consent unto us for to dwell with us, to be one people, if every male among us be circumcised, as they are circumcised.

23) Shall not their cattle and their substance and every beast of their's be our's? only let us consent unto them, and they will dwell with us.

24) And unto Hamor and unto Shechem his son hearkened all that went out of the gate of his city; and every male was circumcised, all that went out of the gate of his city.

25) And it came to pass on the third day, when they were sore (the men were sore due to the circumcision), that two of the sons of Jacob, **Simeon and Levi, Dinah's brethren, took each man his sword, and came upon the city boldly, and slew all the males.**

26) **And they (Dinah's brothers) slew Hamor and Shechem his son with the edge of the sword, and took Dinah out of Shechem's house, and went out.**

27) **The sons of Jacob came upon the slain, and spoiled the city, because they had defiled their sister.**

28) **They took their sheep, and their oxen, and their asses, and that which was in the city, and that which was in the field,**

29) **And all their wealth, and all their little ones, and their wives took they captive, and spoiled even all that was in the house.**

30) **And Jacob said to Simeon and Levi, Ye have troubled me to make me to stink among the inhabitants of the land, among the Canaanites and the Perizzites: and I being few in number, they shall gather themselves together against me, and slay me; and I shall be destroyed, I and my house.**

31) **And they said, Should he deal with our sister as with an harlot? (Dinah's brother never heard a word or listened to a thing the King or Prince said, their anger blinded them. They**

**had their minds made up before anyone even started talking and
they conspired to kill the men. Dinah was going to be a Princess
and later a Queen**)

7) Cursed be their anger, for it was fierce (more force than necessary
to do the job. If you have read my book MATHEW'S WORD
'TWO':REAL WORD OF GOD BIBLE, you remember what
Heavenly Angel Lay Lay said about anger being good, but using
only as much force as necessary to do the job); and their wrath, for it
was cruel: I will divide them in Jacob, and scatter them in Israel.

8) Judah, thou art he (the one) whom thy (your) brethren (brothers)
shall praise: thy hand shall be in the neck of thine enemies; thy
father's children shall bow down before thee.

9) Judah is a lion's whelp: from the prey, my son, thou art gone up:
he stooped down, he couched as a lion, and as an old lion; who shall
rouse him up?

10) The sceptre shall not depart from Judah, nor a lawgiver from
between his feet, until Shiloh come; and unto him shall the gathering
of the people be.

11) Binding his foal unto the vine, and his ass's colt unto the choice
vine; he washed his garments in wine, and his clothes in the blood of
grapes:

12) His eyes shall be red with wine, and his teeth white with milk.

13) Zebulun shall dwell at the haven of the sea (a seaman); and he
shall be for an haven of ships (captain); and his border shall be unto
Zidon.

14) Issachar is a strong ass couching down between two burdens:

15) And he saw that rest was good, and the land that it was pleasant;
and bowed his shoulder to bear, and became a servant unto tribute.

16) Dan shall judge his people, as one of the tribes of Israel.

17) Dan shall be a serpent by the way, an adder in the path, that
biteth the horse heels, so that his rider shall fall backward.

18) I have waited for thy salvation, O LORD.

19) Gad, a troop shall overcome him: but he shall overcome at the
last.

20) Out of Asher his bread shall be fat, and he shall yield royal
dainties.

21) Naphtali is a hind let loose: he giveth goodly words.

22) Joseph is a fruitful bough, even a fruitful bough by a well; whose branches run over the wall:

23) The archers have sorely grieved him, and shot at him, and hated him:

24) But his bow abode in strength, and the arms of his hands were made strong by the hands of the mighty God of Jacob; (from thence is the shepherd, the stone of Israel:)

25) Even by the God of thy father, who shall help thee; and by the Almighty, who shall bless thee with blessings of heaven above, blessings of the deep that lieth under, blessings of the breasts, and of the womb:

26) The blessings of thy father have prevailed above the blessings of my progenitors (ancestors) unto the utmost bound of the everlasting hills: they shall be on the head of Joseph, and on the crown of the head of him that was separate from his brethren.

27) Benjamin shall ravin as a wolf: in the morning he shall devour the prey, and at night he shall divide the spoil.

28) All these are the twelve tribes of Israel: and this is it that their father spake unto them, and blessed them; every one according to his blessing he blessed them.

29) And he (Jacob) charged them (the brothers), and said unto them (the brothers), I am to be gathered unto my people: bury me with my fathers in the cave that is in the field of Ephron the Hittite,

30) In the cave that is in the field of Machpelah, which is before Mamre, in the land of Canaan, which Abraham bought with the field of Ephron the Hittite for a possession of a buryingplace.

31) There they buried Abraham and Sarah his wife; there they buried Isaac and Rebekah his wife; and there I buried Leah.

32) The purchase of the field and of the cave that is therein was from the children of Heth.

33) And when Jacob had made an end of commanding his sons, he gathered up his feet into the bed, and yielded up the ghost, and was gathered unto his people. (Jacob died)

GENESIS 50:1-26

1) And Joseph fell upon his father's face, and wept upon him (Jacob), and kissed him (Jacob, Joseph's departed father).

2) And Joseph commanded his servants the physicians to embalm his father: and the physicians embalmed Israel.

3) And forty days were fulfilled for him; for so are fulfilled the days of those which are embalmed: and the Egyptians mourned for him threescore and ten days (70 days).

4) And when the days of his mourning were past, Joseph spake unto the house of Pharaoh, saying, If now I have found grace in your eyes, speak, I pray you, in the ears of Pharaoh, saying,

5) My father made me swear, saying, Lo, I die: in my grave which I have digged for me in the land of Canaan, there shalt thou bury me. Now therefore let me go up, I pray thee, and bury my father, and I will come again.

6) And Pharaoh said, Go up, and bury thy (your) father, according as he (Jacob) made thee (you) swear.

7) And Joseph went up to bury his father: and with him went up all the servants of Pharaoh, the elders of his house, and all the elders of the land of Egypt,

8) And all the house of Joseph, and his brethren, and his father's house: only their little ones (the children), and their flocks, and their herds, they left in the land of Goshen.

9) And there went up with him (Joseph) both chariots and horsemen: and it was a very great company.

10) And they came to the threshingfloor of Atad, which is beyond Jordan, and there they mourned with a great and very sore lamentation (grief): and he made a mourning for his father seven days.

11) And when the inhabitants of the land, the Canaanites, saw the mourning in the floor of Atad, they said, This is a grievous mourning to the Egyptians: wherefore the name of it was called Abelmizraim, which is beyond Jordan.

12) And his (Jacob) sons did unto him (Jacob) according as he (Jacob) commanded them (Jacob's sons):

13) For his sons carried him (Jacob) into the land of Canaan, and buried him in the cave of the field of Machpelah, which Abraham bought with the field for a possession of a buryingplace of Ephron the Hittite, before Mamre.

14) And Joseph returned into Egypt, he, and his brethren, and all

that went up with him to bury his father, after he had buried his father.

15) And when Joseph's brethren saw that their father was dead, they said, Joseph will peradventure hate us, and will certainly requite us all the evil which we did unto him.

16) And they (Joseph's brothers) sent a messenger unto Joseph, saying, Thy father did command before he died, saying,

17) So shall ye say unto Joseph, Forgive, I pray thee now, the trespass of thy brethren, and their sin; for they did unto thee evil: and now, we pray thee, forgive the trespass of the servants of the God of thy father. And Joseph wept when they spake unto him. (Joseph's brothers are already back at their deceitfulness)

18) And his brethren also went and fell down before his face; and they said, Behold, we be thy (your) servants.

19) And Joseph said unto them, Fear not: for am I in the place of God?

20) But as for you, ye (you) thought evil against me; but God meant it unto good, to bring to pass, as it is this day, to save much people alive.

21) Now therefore fear ye not: I will nourish you, and your little ones. And he comforted them, and spake kindly unto them.

22) And Joseph dwelt in Egypt, he, and his father's house: and Joseph lived an hundred and ten years.

23) And Joseph saw Ephraim's children of the third generation: the children also of Machir the son of Manasseh were brought up upon Joseph's knees.

24) And Joseph said unto his brethren, I die: and God will surely visit you, and bring you out of this land unto the land which he sware to Abraham, to Isaac, and to Jacob.

25) And Joseph took an oath of the children of Israel, saying, God will surely visit you, and ye (you) shall carry up my bones from hence (here).

26) So **Joseph** died, being an **hundred and ten years old** (110 years old): and they (Joseph's children and relatives) embalmed him (Joseph), and he (Joseph) was put in a coffin in Egypt.

(END OF GENESIS)

MOSES

MOSES

Exodus 1:1-22

1) Now these are the names of the children of Israel, which came into Egypt; every man and his household came with Jacob.

2) Reuben, Simeon, Levi, and Judah,

3) Issachar, Zebulun, and Benjamin,

4) Dan, and Naphtali, Gad, and Asher.

5) And all the souls that came out of the loins of Jacob were seventy souls (70 people): for Joseph was in Egypt already.

6) And Joseph died, and all his brethren, and all that generation. (the whole generation of Joseph died off, just like every generation that does something dramatically good or evil, it's the whole generation who either profits or suffers and three generations after them)

7) And the children of Israel were fruitful, and increased abundantly, and multiplied, and waxed exceeding mighty; and the land was filled with them.

8) Now there arose up a new king over Egypt, which knew not Joseph.

9) And he (the new King) said unto his people, Behold, the people of the children of Israel are more and mightier than we:

10) Come on, let us deal wisely with them (the children of Israel/Jacob. Remember, Jacob and Israel is the same man. His name was Jacob before 'Jacob's Ladder', then God changed his name to Israel); lest they (the children of Israel) multiply, and it come to pass, that, when there falleth out any war, they (the children of Israel) join also unto our enemies, and fight against us, and so get them (the children of Israel) up out of the land.

11) Therefore they (the Egyptians) did set over them (the children of Israel) taskmasters to afflict them (the children of Israel) with their (the Egyptians) burdens (what burdens do the Egyptians have? Manual labor). And they (the children of Israel) built for Pharaoh treasure cities, Pithom and Raamses.

12) But the more they (the Egyptians) afflicted them (the children of Israel), the more they (the children of Israel) multiplied and grew. And they (the Egyptians) were grieved because of the children of Israel.

13) And the Egyptians made the children of Israel to serve with rigour [1.

use of demanding standards: the application of precise and exacting standards in the doing of something. 2. lack of tolerance: severity, strictness, or harshness in dealing with somebody. 3. hardship: great hardship or difficulty. (Encarta ® World English Dictionary © & (P) 1998-2004 Microsoft Corporation. All rights reserved.)]:

14) And they (the Egyptians) made their (the Israelites) lives bitter with hard bondage, in morter, and in brick, and in all manner of service in the field: all their service, wherein they (the Egyptians) made them (the Israelites) serve, was with rigour [1. use of demanding standards: the application of precise and exacting standards in the doing of something. 2. lack of tolerance: severity, strictness, or harshness in dealing with somebody. 3. hardship: great hardship or difficulty. (Encarta ® World English Dictionary © & (P) 1998-2004 Microsoft Corporation. All rights reserved.)].

15) And the king of Egypt spake to the Hebrew midwives, of which the name of the one was Shiphrah, and the name of the other Puah:

16) And he (the king of Egypt) said, When ye (you) do the office of a midwife to the Hebrew women, and see them (the Israelite women giving birth) upon the stools; if it be a son, then ye (you) shall kill him (the Israelite son): but if it be a daughter, then she (the Israelite daughter) shall live.

17) But the midwives feared God, and did not as the king of Egypt commanded them, but saved the men children alive (smart women, they feared God more than any human man).

18) And the king of Egypt called for the midwives, and said unto them (the midwives), Why have ye (you) done this thing, and have saved the men children alive?

19) And the midwives said unto Pharaoh, Because the Hebrew women are not as the Egyptian women; for they (the Hebrew women) are lively, and are delivered ere [before: before or earlier in time than. (Encarta ® World English Dictionary © & (P) 1998-2004 Microsoft Corporation. All rights reserved.)] the midwives come in unto them (the Hebrew women don't need help with the delivery of the babies like the Egyptian women do. The Hebrew women aren't 'chicken' and don't complain like the Egyptian women do. The Hebrew women have already delivered by the time the midwives get to them unlike they Egyptian women need toe midwives to help them deliver the children)

20) Therefore God dealt well with the midwives (like I said before, 'smart women those midwives'):   and the people multiplied, and waxed [increase: to increase in size, power, or intensity (Encarta ® World English Dictionary © & (P) 1998-2004 Microsoft Corporation. All rights reserved.)] very mighty.

21) And it came to pass (in time) (have you ever noticed God never blesses right away? He always blesses 'in time', once we prove ourselves to Him, He blesses us), because the midwives feared God, that he (God) made them (the midwives) houses [1. occupants of a house: all of the people who are in a house at one time, particularly the people who usually live there. 2. community dwelling: a building in which a community of people lives. (Encarta ® World English Dictionary © & (P) 1998-2004 Microsoft Corporation. All rights reserved.)]

22) And Pharaoh charged (commanded) all his people (his whole kingdom), saying, Every son that is born ye shall cast into the river, and every daughter ye shall save alive.

Exodus 2:1-25

1) And there went a man of the house of Levi, and took to wife a daughter of Levi.

2) And the woman conceived, and bare a son: and when she (the mother) saw him (her son) that he (her son) was a goodly child, she (the mother) hid him (the son) three months.

3) And when she (the mother) could not longer hide him (he was getting too big and demanding more of her time and attention, he was growing), she (the mother) took for him (the son) an ark [2. sanctuary: a place providing refuge. (Encarta ® World English Dictionary © & (P) 1998-2004 Microsoft Corporation. All rights reserved.)] of bulrushes [1. waterside plant: a plant that grows in wet conditions, with leaves like grass and clusters of drooping brown flowers. Genus: Scirpus 2. U.K. tall marsh plant with brown heads: a tall marsh plant with brown furry flower spikes. Genus: Typha 3. bible papyrus: in the Bible, a papyrus plant.   (Encarta ® World English Dictionary © & (P) 1998-2004 Microsoft Corporation. All rights reserved.), and daubed it (the ark of bulrushes) with slime and with pitch, and put the child (her son) therein (inside the ark of bulrushes); and she (the Hebrew woman) laid it (the ark) in the flags [most important of group: the most important or prestigious

among a group of similar and related things. (Encarta ® World English Dictionary © & (P) 1998-2004 Microsoft Corporation. All rights reserved.)] by the river's brink [edge of something: the very edge of something, for example, a steep drop or a riverbank Encarta ® World English Dictionary © & (P) 1998-2004 Microsoft Corporation. All rights reserved.)].

4) And his (the baby boys) sister stood afar off, to wit [intelligence: mental acumen, intelligence, or reasoning power. (Encarta ® World English Dictionary © & (P) 1998-2004 Microsoft Corporation. All rights reserved.)] what would be done to him (the Hebrew child).

5) And the daughter of Pharaoh came down to wash herself at the river; and her maidens walked along by the river's side; and when she (the Pharaoh's daughter) saw the ark among the flags, she sent her maid to fetch it (God forbid someone of royalty get wet. She had to send her maid to get the ark. I wonder if Hagar had that problem. Hagar was also the Pharaoh's daughter during the time of Abram, remember? Hagar was a princess of Egypt before she became Sarai's handmaid. What a demotion for Hagar. One minute Hagar is the Princess of Egypt in Royalty, the next minute Hagar is a slave for an Israelite woman, Sarai, in poverty).

6) And when she (the Pharaoh's daughter) had opened it, she (the Pharaoh's daughter) saw the child (the Hebrew boy): and, behold, the babe wept. And she (the Pharaoh's daughter) had compassion on him (the Hebrew infant boy), and said, This is one of the Hebrews' children.

7) Then said his (the Hebrew infant boy's) sister to Pharaoh's daughter, Shall I go and call to thee (you) a nurse of the Hebrew women, that she (the Hebrew woman) may nurse the child for thee (you)?

8) And Pharaoh's daughter said to her, Go. And the maid went and called the child's mother (cool huh? The infant's mother is going to nurse her own son).

9) And Pharaoh's daughter said unto her (the infant's mother), Take this child away, and nurse it for me, and I will give thee thy wages (now the infant's own mother is not only nursing her own son, but also getting paid to nurse her own son by an Egyptian Princess). And the women (the infant's mother) took the child, and nursed it.

10) And the child grew, and she (the infant's mother) brought him unto Pharaoh's daughter, and he became her son. And she called his name Moses: and she (the Pharaoh's daughter) said, Because I drew him out of

the water.

11) And it came to pass in those days, when Moses was grown, that he went out unto his brethren, and looked on their (the Hebrew's) burdens: and he (Moses) spied an Egyptian smiting (hitting) an Hebrew, one of his brethren (brothers).

12) And he (Moses) looked this way and that way, and when he (Moses) saw that there was no man, he (Moses) slew (killed) the Egyptian, and hid him (the Egyptian) in the sand.

13) And when he (Moses) went out the second day, behold, two men of the Hebrews strove together: and he (Moses) said to him (the man) that did the wrong, Wherefore smitest thou thy fellow?

14) And he (the man) said, Who made thee (you) a prince and a judge over us? intendest thou to kill me, as thou killedst the Egyptian? And Moses feared, and said, Surely this thing is known.

15) Now when Pharaoh heard this thing, he sought to slay Moses. But Moses fled from the face of Pharaoh, and dwelt in the land of Midian: and he (Moses) sat down by a well.

16) Now the priest of Midian had seven daughters: and they (the daughters) came and drew water, and filled the troughs to water their father's flock.

17) And the shepherds came and drove them away: but Moses stood up and helped them (the daughters), and watered their flock.

18) And when they (the daughters) came to Reuel their father, he (Reuel) said, How is it that ye are come so soon to day? (Why are you back so soon?)

19) And they (the daughters) said, An Egyptian delivered us out of the hand of the shepherds, and also drew water enough for us, and watered the flock.

20) And he (Reuel) said unto his daughters, And where is he (the man)? why is it that ye have left the man? call him (the man), that he (the man) may eat bread.

21) And Moses was content to dwell with the man: and he (Reuel) gave Moses Zipporah his daughter.

22) And she (Zipporah) bare him (Moses) a son, and he (Moses) called his (the son) name Gershom: for he said, I have been a stranger in a strange land.

23) And it came to pass in process of time, that the king of Egypt died:

and the children of Israel sighed by reason of the bondage, and they cried, and their cry came up unto God by reason of the bondage.

24) And **God heard their groaning, and God remembered his covenant with Abraham, with Isaac, and with Jacob.**

25) And God looked upon the children of Israel, **and God had respect unto them.** (sometimes we have to plead and plead when we go to God for Him to step in and respect us)

(CONTINUED IN:
HEAVENLY ANGEL LAY LAY
EXPLAINS WHY CHILDREN AND SPORTS
ARE DEFINITELY A RELIGION
IN TODAY'S SOCIETY)

BIBLIOGRAPHY

1. Encarta ® World English Dictionary © & (P) 1998-2004 Microsoft Corporation. All rights reserved.

2. Merriam Webster's Collegiate Dictionary Tenth Edition (1993), United States of America.

3. The Holy Bible King James Version (1998), B. B. Kirkbride Bible Co., Inc. Indianapolis, IN..USA